PAINTING WITH POETRY

A POETIC MEMOIR

MJ JENNETTI

© 2021 by MJ Jennetti and GiGi Whitt

All rights reserved, including the right to reproduce or copy this book, or any portions of it, in any form whatsoever without written permission.

Published in the USA by
Foxwood Hill Press

DEDICATION

To my husband Tony and daughter Theresa with love and appreciation.

TABLE OF CONTENTS

Introduction	1
Two Art Forms	5
Painting With Poetry	6
Poetry in Motion	8
Childhood Memories	11
Childhood Memories	12
Grandparents' Place	15
Those were the Days	18
Bay View Memories	20
Places Near and Far	23
A Time Long Gone	24
Home of Fifty Years	27
Humboldt County	29
Unique Town of Eureka	31
Trinidad	34
Lebanon Home	36
Apple Hill	39

Monterey Memories	41
Remembering Yosemite	44
Magnificent Alaska	47
Paradise Found	49
Wondrous Yellowstone	51
Place of Red Rock	54
European Adventures	56
Random Thoughts	**59**
Perilous Pandemic	60
Red Sky at Morning	62
Rebuilding	64
Communing With the Earth	66
Sunshine	68
Windy Days	70
Thoughts on a Rainy Day	72
Fear of Heights	74

The Love of Reading	76
More Thoughts About Rain	78
Stargazing	80
Friendships	82
The Joy of Gifting	84
Stuff of Dreams	86
Internet Connections	88
Reunions Revisited	90
My Fifth Appendage	93
Missed My Calling?	95
Peddling Away	97
On Turning 75	99
Reflections on a Marriage	101
Muffin	104

Keeping the Faith	107
Keeping the Faith	108

One Child	111
A Dark Place	113
Poetic Memoir	115
One Final Thought	117
Acknowledgements	119
About the Artist	120
About the Author	121

INTRODUCTION

Painting With Poetry is my attempt to revive an interest that I had as a child. During my early years, I enjoyed writing poetry, and once wrote a term paper on Shakespeare in iambic pentameter. Back then I was not into writing free verse poetry, thinking that most poems should rhyme. My interest in free verse took shape through attending a poetry club once at my church and hearing poems read by members there. Even then it was a long time before I actually started composing my own, the result of which is this book. The poems here are a collection of thoughts and experiences I have had over the years as well as my hope for the future. Writing them has afforded me the opportunity to relive parts of my life and reflect upon them. I recall some events with great joy and others with some sadness. However that is the way life is, being a combination of both hills and valleys. Writing these poems has been a memorable journey for me, and as I say in one of them, can serve as my memoir.

The book is divided into five parts:

"Two Art Forms," describes how my poems relate to the two art forms of painting on canvas and writing on paper. Here I also have tried to show how my poetry evolves.

"Childhood Memories," describes places where I have lived and visited while growing up and thoughts I have about those times.

"Places Near and Far," includes the different

locals I have visited over the years.

"Random Thoughts," contains my musings on various topics.

"Keeping the Faith," touches upon my religious leanings and some things that have impacted my Christian faith.

TWO ART FORMS

PAINTING WITH POETRY

Poetry resembles a painting,
Putting pen to paper like a brush to canvas.
Both are subjective and intimately personal.
Both can create a mood,
through the color of paint and the color of words.
Both can evoke many feelings: fear, courage,
happiness, sorrow, pain, healing, light, darkness.
Each can convey realism
and likewise the abstract.
An impressionistic painting,
such as one by Monet, can convey both.
Scenes bathed in light draw us to a place
both familiar and unfamiliar.
A western one by Remington is more concrete.

Many years ago I tried my hand at painting,
copying pictures I would find.
My aim was to make them similar to a photograph
leaving out the abstract element.

Mysteriously that was not always the finished product.

Someone saw a human skull in the clouds of one painting.

A close look revealed it to be there.

Art, be it painting or poetry, can sometimes lead to the unexpected.

Poetry like painting can open up thoughts and imagination, and

can enrich our lives in unforeseen ways.

Both can be linked together as valued treasures.

POETRY IN MOTION

I have always enjoyed walking.
Connecting with nature, meditating, relieving stress,
walking is the great healer.
It's also been a way for me to create poetry.
When I start to walk my mind is a blank canvas
which gradually takes on color
as I paint upon it with words.
Ideas begin to form as I continue walking,
creating a picture in my mind.
Returning home I set my thoughts to paper
as a painter would do on canvas.
Both art forms create an image which is subjective to the beholder.
We can like what we see or read or decide otherwise.

People's tastes differ which makes life interesting.
How boring it would be if we all thought alike.
Now that I am in my seventh decade,
my poems are both a memoir and a mirror into the future,

recalling both my youth and what may be to come.

Both evoke happiness and sadness, courage and fear.

Walking, staying in motion and creating poetry is positive.

Life does not stand still; it is forever in motion, forever changing.

The challenge is to move with it,

being grateful for its trials as well as its rewards.

Poetry in motion is poetry flowing through the mind's eye,

creating its own river of blessings.

CHILDHOOD MEMORIES

CHILDHOOD MEMORIES

Growing up in Ohio well over seventy years ago,

it was a different time, a different place, a different world:

No internet, no cell phones

Only three channels on a black and white TV with a temperamental screen prone to rolling or plagued by static

It was a simpler time, a safer time.

We walked to school alone as kids, no parents in tow:

Mother's homemade popcorn balls on Halloween

No fear of razor blades in Trick-or-Treat bags

No fear of going alone door-to-door decked out in costumes

No video games just sitting on a couch

We made up our own games instead:

Playing outside, acting out our favorite characters

like the Lone Ranger or Roy Rogers

Making forts out of tall bushes

Pretending a wagon was a stagecoach,

the sidewalk a dusty trail heading overland

Going to the local movie theater on a Saturday afternoon

Buying a ten cent bag of popcorn which you could hold in your fist

Trembling in fright watching, "Creature from the Black Lagoon"

Running out of the theater during a showing of "The Thing"

Simple birthday parties with no jump houses or other trappings, just some cake, ice cream and simple games

Junk food had yet to make the scene, and there was far less obesity.

Few mothers worked, so home cooked meals were in fashion.

But it was not always a rosy time, seen only through tinted glasses.

Women started to feel frustrated, resentful of just being at home.

Times started changing as I neared adulthood,

and never were the same again.

Maybe I saw things through the eyes of a child,

never sensing the unsettled feelings that gripped the older.

It's common for us to look back in longing,

if our childhood is idyllic, if everything is grounded, if

everything seems well.

But even then not all was as it might have seemed.

The changing times are testament to that,

with no turning back the clock.

We long for our youth, when we could take two stairs at a time,

when a fall just meant getting right back up on the bike,

when we could hike for hours and never tire:

No aches and pains, no worry about meeting Father Time

Childhood was not always worry free,

but I can look back and say it was all too fleeting, yet sublime.

GRANDPARENTS' PLACE

My grandparents' place was magical,

long time home of my paternal grandparents built in 1917.

My dad was 14 when they came there along with his older and younger brother.

Before that Granddad had been a tenant farmer,

moving ten times in my dad's 14 years.

Dad kept a list of them all which I loved hearing him recite.

My grandmother would remain there for 47 more years,

eternally grateful for a permanent home.

Granddad planted an elm tree out front which grew to great height,

until Dutch elm disease claimed it, and it had to be cut down.

Planted shrubs became a forest.

How I loved wandering through them as a child,

pretending I was in a jungle or some other mysterious place.

We would set out early making the eight hour trip,

along the two-lane highway,

passing through the many small towns along the way,

before the interstate went in, and we never saw them again.

Seeing my grandmother standing in her driveway,

straight out of Norman Rockwell, holding a gift for me,

my grandparents' home was magical.

Sitting on the big front porch, gliding back and forth on the swing,

playing with toys stored in a box there was a little morsel of heaven.

Granddad hung a swing from a tree branch,

where I could swing to my heart's delight.

The memories are endless:

Waking up in the little pink bedroom with its sloped ceiling

Hearing the rooster crow next door

Hurrying downstairs to the smell of bacon and pancakes

Listening to my uncle play his violin and Dad the piano

Festive dinners around the dining room table,

where there was always an extra plate set for guests

My grandparents' home was a magical place,
Before my grandfather passed away,
before my grandmother fell into depression,
and people stopped coming to visit.
Gone are the vestiges of the past.
The field next door is no more,
and buildings stand in its place.
The home no longer looks the same,
but in my mind's eye it will remain forever magical,
another treasure safely locked away
with other jewels from my childhood.

THOSE WERE THE DAYS

Looking through my old high school yearbook of 1964,
I realize how much things have changed.
It was a totally different time and place,
with styles that speak of another era.
I don't know when I became fully aware of this,
suddenly realizing how dated everything had become.
Strict dress codes were enforced,
unlike today when almost anything goes.

I never wore jeans or anything resembling them,
only dresses or skirts and sweaters.
Silk stockings and black "slipper flats,"
were all the rage in high school,
not necessarily being the best type of footware
during frigid, snowy Ohio weather:
No baggy pants for boys,
No tee shirts with logos

No ripped jeans or stressed jackets,
No athletic shoes or sneakers
School hours were much longer with study halls
taking up two periods a day.
I never seemed to study much in them,
just sat worrying about an upcoming test,
especially if it was an algebra one,
math never being my forte.
Our school had its cliques, and I was never in a popular one,
but I made some lasting friendships
which have endured through the years.

Sitting in a classroom today would be much different,
yet in some ways it would be the same.
Navigating though those years has never been easy,
never without its pain for any generation.
Many in my class of over 500 students,
never remained connected in any way after graduation.
For them, as for me, there was life after high school.
I painted a different picture on my life's future canvas,
and reaped the rewards that came my way.
Turning the pages on my old yearbook takes me back,
but I'm forever grateful that I moved forward.

BAY VIEW MEMORIES

Bay View, Michigan, lovely summer resort area,
next to Petoskey on Little Traverse Bay beside Lake Michigan,
home to beautiful restored Victorian era cottages,
long connected to the United Methodist Church.
I was about eight years old when I first went there,
visiting my cousins and staying at the Terrace Inn.
What memories abide there at this treasured place.
Built in 1911, it was an extended stay destination
for many older adults, some retired ministers.

I would spend many summers there swimming in the lake,
enjoying countless activities during the Bay View Music Festival.
Opera, theater, chamber music, recitals and more,
my interest in music was cultivated there.
Movies in the evening, youth programs during the day,

the list was endless.

I approached our week's stay with great anticipation.

We rose well before dawn to beat the military caravans,

traveling north along the two-lane highway to Grayling, Michigan.

What joy at seeing Lake Michigan appear over a hill!

Remembering my uncle playing shuffleboard each morning

My aunt and parents visiting in the hotel lobby

Hearing my cousin announce,"It's 67 degrees"

Lake Michigan can be very cold indeed!

Diving off the pier into the frigid water, my body going numb

Youth has a higher inner thermostat.

Treacherous hidden undertows can sweep one out to sea.

But youth is immortal to such dangers, immune to aging's inexorable advance.

Working at the Terrace Inn during college:

Going to beach parties at night and having one two many hangovers

Eating pie at Jesperson's and downing sundaes at the local malt shop

My last time there was over 20 years ago.

The inn's former owners have long since passed away,

and the place bears no resemblance to that earlier time.

I prefer to remember it the way it was so many years ago.

Time brings many changes, but the past remains painted in my mind,

full of wondrous colors on a treasured canvas.

PLACES NEAR AND FAR

A TIME LONG GONE

I well remember Sunnyvale and surrounding cities,

when it was a much more rural area.

Gone was the Valley of the Heart's Delight,

when we came there in 1970,

but it still was much different than it is today.

Sunnyvale was just a small town along Murphy Street,

home to Hart's Department Store and a few other shops.

These gave way to the Sunnyvale Town Center,

an indoor mall, the likes of which were becoming more popular.

I well recall the Libby's cannery,

with its iconic Libby's can rising high above it.

Mornings would reveal numerous workers,

walking up the road towards the cannery buildings,

now long gone, and just a part of history.

Gradually more changes came to Sunnyvale.

The mall was torn down, and for years the city stood in limbo.

Developers argued the best way to move forward.
Eventually that meant constructing high rise buildings,
along with some expensive shops and restaurants.
Sunnyvale as I once knew it was no longer recognizable.

Surrounding cities suffered the same fate.
Vallco Town Center in Cupertino was demolished,
and once more developers argued with the city
about the best way to move forward.
Now it is following the same track as Sunnyvale,
creating a city within a city of shops, housing and restaurants.
The monstrous behemoth in San Jose called Santana Row,
is forever expanding and sending out its tentacles
to consume more land surrounding it.
How fondly I recall how it once was,
long before it morphed into what it is today.

Yes, the changes have been many since 1970,
and I remember that time long ago,
when I was young and things were simpler,
but time moves on, things change,
some for the better, and others for the worse.
Life is like that, always painting new landscapes.

There is joy in embracing new horizons, and seeing where they lead,

using the best colors from the artist's palette.

HOME OF FIFTY YEARS

What is it like to live in a home for fifty years?

What memories are stored there?

Many happy, some sad, all pieces of a greater whole

I was 24 when we came to this place,

brand new home, original owners my husband and I.

Nothing but dirt surrounded it,

no lawn, no trees, nothing but tract homes lining the street.

Most of us were young homesteaders just beginning our adult lives.

A 30-year mortgage could only be imagined,

the years an interminable stretch ahead.

But Father Time is forever the magician,

performing his tricks, speeding up the clock.

Our street became lined with trees,

and our homes surrounded by shrubs.

Old landscaping was replaced by new.

Homes became personalized with different roofs and additions.

Memories abound at this home:

Countless parties at Christmas, birthdays, anniversaries

Suddenly we were aware of the years advancing ever more quickly.

Children have grown and gone.

Only a couple of original homesteaders remain.

The rest have moved away,

or passed into the next life that awaits us all.

After fifty years we also left,

moving to Eureka along the magnificent North Coast.

Many call it the Lost Coast, but for us it is something found.

Now in our senior years we look back to that departed home

knowing that it will forever remain locked in our treasure chest.

HUMBOLDT COUNTY

Roughly 300 miles north of San Francisco,

lies a jewel in California's storied terrain:

Humboldt County, home to the magnificent Lost Coast,

with its wild and wind powered waves,

crashing against rocks and jetties with unrelenting force

Home to breathtaking redwood forests and high mountains,

where pillows of fog rest against a bed frame of hills

Leaving the Bay Area with its hectic highways,

crowded cities and ever increasing urban sprawl,

one is transported into another world of welcome serenity.

Small towns scattered between farmland and open water,

where herds of deer can suddenly appear,

lend a sense of peace to all who draw near.

Humboldt County is home to Eureka,

with its famous Carson House and sister Pink Lady,

where its sparkling harbor, galleries, and hand painted murals,

create memorable charm in the artistic Old Town.

Hopeful writers congregate in coffee shops,

and musicians pop up on street corners to serenade listening ears.

Local artists find home for their creations.

Bookstores lure the wishful reader,

and waterfront trails call out to ambitious hikers.

Humboldt County is a wild and often mysterious place,

captivating visitors with its quiet grace.

Weather can suddenly take a turn with wind and rain taking hold,

powering up the stormy seas only to return to calm,

as sun peeks through, and rains then ease.

Nature paints a glorious sky, and rainbows stretch across the clouds,

which open up to splash blue where once was gray.

I have come to call this place home.

Memories abound in my former place of fifty years,

but new ones are being forged in another time,

nothing short of wonderment, nothing short of sublime.

UNIQUE TOWN OF EUREKA

We moved to Eureka right before the perilous pandemic of 2020,
having visited here many times over the years.
After living 50 years in the Bay Area
with its ever increasing traffic and urban sprawl,
we were ready to escape to a more peaceful place.
We have found it in Eureka
with its beautiful redwood forests, open water areas
and definitive rural feel.

Located right along the spectacular Lost Coast,
Eureka has its special set of treasures.
The Waterfront is home to many boats,
and kayakers are often seen rowing away.
The Old Town has many wonderful galleries and shops,
with Old Town Coffee and Chocolates
being a gathering place for writers and caffeine addicts.

Bookstores, both new and used, cater to the reader.

Many fine restaurants, bakeries and creameries

beckon to those with appetites.

Thrift stores and consignment shops

draw those who don't care to deplete their bank accounts.

Many buildings, especially those along Opera Alley,

have colorful murals painted by local artists.

The same is true for the many utility boxes

which have become a showplace for the artist's palette.

Eureka for the most part is an old town,

founded in 1850, and incorporated in 1856.

Many of the famous Victorian homes still stand,

the most famous being the Carson House and Pink Lady,

however they have many companions throughout Eureka.

Newer subdivisions exist, but it's the old that stand out.

Eureka has something for everyone.

Hiking and biking trails abound.

Sequoia Park with its zoo and newly completed Sky Walk

upon which visitors can brave the heights,

and look out high above the redwood forest,

are just some of the many attractions.

There is a peacefulness here.

Just a short drive takes one into the country,

peppered by organic produce gardens and grazing animals.

The forests are everywhere, both in and out of town.

Beaches beckon those who love the seashore.

Eureka has become my new and lasting home.

Years of living in the Bay Area

are fast becoming a distant memory.

Even though its images will be forever

painted upon my mind's canvas,

I have created new pictures heading into the future.

TRINIDAD

Few coastal areas are more beautiful
than the small town of Trinidad, California,
known for its magnificent seashore and numerous trails
winding through forested areas with scenic outcroppings.
On a clear day the sky is vibrant blue,
as is the ocean with its white caps and sandy beaches.
Wildflowers bloom in colorful abundance,
teasing the artist's palette and the photographer's camera.
Seabirds soar above, ever darting back and forth
to catch a fish or land on the pier.
Rabbits, squirrels and other small creatures
make their home along the wooded trails.

Famous for its iconic lighthouse and Memorial Cross,
Trinidad pays tribute to those lost at sea.
Crab boats can be seen in the calm harbor,
and visitors tempt fish to catch their bait.
Lovely seafront homes dot the small village,

windows opening out to glorious views.

Trinidad offers peace and renewal, a place to meditate,

and find serenity in a challenging world.

Even on stormy days when the wind kicks up the waves,

and the sky is gray with dark clouds,

Trinidad has its magic and its continuing lure.

The Creator lives and speaks here to all who choose to listen.

His presence graces this place with all His glory!

LEBANON HOME

Lebanon, Pennsylvania, is my husband's childhood home.

Small Pennsylvania Dutch town,

nestled in the surrounding corn fields and rolling hills,

on the eastern side of the state,

it dates back to Revolutionary times.

Lined with streets of row houses and narrow alley ways,

it was home to the once thriving Bethlehem Steel, now long gone.

Only empty buildings with broken windows remain,

scattered among tall weeds near the railroad tracks.

Trains still pass through daily,

whistles sounding sharply at crossings,

heard clearly at my husband's childhood home.

I was 22 when I first visited there.

It was Thanksgiving, and I traveled through the night,

with my soon-to-be husband Tony.

Festive dinner where I first sampled my mother-in-law's chicken ravioli

Family and friends gathered around the dining room table

I will visit there for 30 more years,

until my mother-in-law's passing.

Recollections are painted viviedly from this place:

  Fond memories of sitting on the front porch swing

  listening to the trains, gently going back and forth

  Fond memories of St. Luke's Church with its

  prominent gargoyles peering out from the roof top

  Fond memories of walking up to 9th and Chestnut

  Streets when it was safe to do so,

  before the town became a more dangerous place

Before stores like Haak Brothers and Pomeroy's became parking lots

Before indoor malls took over in outlying areas

Before time erased what once was sacred

It's been over 20 years,

Since I have been back to my husband's childhood home.

Another family is there now,

and the house is not the same.

Memories are now painted on my mind's canvas, and treasures are stored up in my heart.

APPLE HILL

Nestled in the hills above the quaint Gold Rush town of Placerville,

lies an enchanting area known as Apple Hill.

Numerous apple farms and orchards are scattered

throughout this wonderful place which I came to love.

Able's Apple Acres has its famous apple dumplings,

made even more scrumptious a la mode with Apple Cinnamon Sauce.

Boa Vista Orchard features great produce and condiments.

Apple butter, jams, dried fruit, nuts, sauces, all are here.

Homemade, pies ready for the oven, are on display.

Outside, crafters show off their creations further tempting the tourist.

Fall is the time to visit Apple Hill, especially around Halloween.

The farms are alive with decorations and pumpkins,

getting everyone in the spirit for this festive holiday.

With Christmas just around the corner,

much of that holiday is featured too.

Apple Hill became an annual destination for my husband and me.

Staying overnight in Placerville, and spending the next morning

sampling wonderful treats, and touring our favorite apple sites,

it will always remain a treasured memory.

Since we are now much further away, our times of going there are no more.

We look forward to finding new places even though we will miss the old.

It's part of life's changes, moving forward.

Looking back with wonderful memories,

we paint new pictures on a forever changing canvas.

MONTEREY MEMORIES

Monterey, California enticed us early on,
and we can recall many wonderful memories there
painted in vivid colors on the mind's canvas.
John Steinbeck used Cannery Row as a backdrop
for his novel by the same name,
forever immortalizing this famous area.
He kept company with another well-known inhabitant,
"Doc" Ed Ricketts, as he was known to the locals.
Having a weakness for alcohol, Ed was killed
when his car stalled on the railroad tracks.
His old office is one of the few remaining
buildings from that former time.

We first visited Monterey and Cannery Row in the early 1970's.

Things were much different then, before it became a mecca for tourists.

The old sardine canneries were long gone, but their spirit remained.

We fondly recall the organ grinder and his famous little monkey

who entertained us for many years at Fisherman's Wharf.

Our daughter loved handing the monkey a coin.

Then one day the duo were gone, never to be seen again.

Many other treasures also disappeared:

The famous Diving Bell our daughter loved to descend

giving a look at the ocean floor just off the wharf

The Edgewater Packing House with its colorful carousel

Hosenfelters with its huge sundaes, malts and shakes

The Wearhouse Restaurant with its famous lobster dinners, including their wonderful soup and salad bar

Then came the Monterey Bay Aquarium along with more tourists.

Things gradually began to change, and the old feeling was lost.

We still enjoyed visiting Monterey, Cannery Row and Carmel.

Abalonetti's on Fisherman's Wharf became a favorite restaurant,

although we would always miss the Wearhouse.

Time has a way of marching on, often to a different drummer.

We preferred the one of old, but that was not to be.

Still, Monterey with it's glorious sea coast and fond memories,

will be with us forever, a beautiful picture to be treasured.

REMEMBERING YOSEMITE

Yosemite National Park is one of California's natural wonders.

An icon to the naturalist John Muir and photographer Ansel Adams,

both immortalized this magical place into the realms of history.

Here are majestic granite cliffs and stunning waterfalls,

crisscrossed by numerous hiking trails teaming with wildlife.

Deer, black bears and cougars lurk in the surrounding woods,

and can make their presence known to the unsuspecting tourist.

I first stepped into Yosemite well over forty years ago,

and have that first image forever imprinted in my mind:

Staying in a tent cabin at Curry village

Dining in the nearby cafeteria

Hiking up the misty trail to Vernal Falls,

taking care not to slip on the wet steps leading to the top

Climbing to the top of Yosemite Falls, foolishly not

taking enough provisions

Drinking from other hikers' canteens in the upper 90-degree heat

Youth is careless in many ways, and can pay the price.

Nights around a campfire listening to a ranger's tales, days exploring Mirror Lake, and the surrounding meadow imprinted lasting memories.

Today it is a mere pool, ever changing and getting smaller.

The grand Ahwahnee Hotel is a centerpiece of Yosemite.

Meaning,"deep grassy valley," to the Miwok Indians,

who once claimed this land as their treasured home,

the Ahwahnee with its rustic architecture is a must see,

one of the grand hotels on a short list of memorable ones.

I last stepped into Yosemite over ten years ago,

traveling with a senior group, my husband and I,

no longer quite as able to go on long hikes

or climb to dangerous areas as age had started to set in.

Father Time was slowing advancing, shaking his fist, claiming his due.

But the magic was still there with

Yosemite Falls thundering down after an all night rain,

sending clouds of mist onto the trail, a full picture of its glory.

It may be my last time seeing Yosemite.

There are new places now to explore in a quiet way,

new places to paint memories onto my mind's canvas.

We are forever growing, changing until the very end.

Then will come the greatest change of all,

within an entirely new realm!

MAGNIFICENT ALASKA

Traveling to Alaska can be a wondrous adventure.
What other state offers towering mountains of ice,
large glaciers, abundant wildlife, and a rich history?
Land of the Midnight Sun,
it can be light for 24 hours,
while just as dark at other times.
Cruising through Glacier Bay,
one views a world dressed in white.
Huge chunks of ice can tumble down,
crashing into the water and churning up waves.

The Aurora Borealis or famous Northern Lights,
can light up the sky in a rainbow of colors,
painting it in shades of green, red and purple.
Mt. McKinley, the highest peak in North America,
better known by its native American name, Denali,
rises high above the earth's surface.
Often shrouded in clouds, it sometimes shines forth revealing its brilliant snow capped peak.

Gold hungry prospectors came here years ago,
some risking life and limb to become wealthy.
The lure of riches can make fools of many.
Native people, or Inuits, still paint
their rich history upon this great land,
holding onto their sacred customs,
and adding another dimension to Alaska's culture.
Traveling here can be an unforgettable experience,
imprinted on the mind's canvas as a treasured memory.

PARADISE FOUND

The island of Hawaii is a true paradise.
Deep blue turquoise water spreads out from sandy beaches,
painting a scene of incredible beauty.
Visiting Maui years ago remains forever
imprinted upon my mind's canvas.
My husband and I spent a glorious week at Kaanapali,
enjoying time at a condo near the beach.

Lahaina, about ten miles from there,
can be quite a bit warmer,
and is home to a huge banyan tree.
Nothing can compare to this most unusual sight.
Standing 60 feet tall, its octopus limbs
include 46 trunks which spread over a large area.
In its early years some of its shoots
turned back downwards into the ground,
creating what is seen today.

We traveled along the Road to Hana,

a roller coaster of twists and turns,

down muddy and treacherous roads.

The 65-mile trip goes along both coast and wild jungle.

We passed by black sandy beaches, waterfalls,

and rich green areas covered with flowers,

where the natural artist was at work,

painting rich colors from his varied palette.

Charles Lindbergh is buried here

on the grounds of a tranquil church,

far away from the adoring crowds that once surrounded him.

Seemed a fitting place for one whose life

was cloaked in both fame and tragedy.

Hawaii has numerous ethnic groups.

Filipino, Japanese, Native Hawaiians and others,

all contribute to its rich culture and heritage.

The famous luaus with their roasted pig,

dancers and music can be the highlight of a visit there.

We will always remember our magical trip to Hawaii,

its picture forever painted in our minds

along with so many other treasures.

WONDROUS YELLOWSTONE

Yellowstone National Park is a veritable wonder,

of unique and breathtaking beauty.

Stretching across Wyoming and parts of Montana and Idaho,

it teems with an abundance of scenery and wildlife.

Bordered by the magnificent high Tetons,

it is famous for its many geysers and thermal areas.

Once every hour Old Faithful

shoots it scalding plume of water high into the sky,

captivating all who come to see it.

Numerous smaller geysers dot the landscape,

along with bubbling mud pots giving off their sulfurous smell.

Vibrant colors spill across the area,

being all shades of the rainbow, an artist's dream.

The famous Opal Pool with its turquoise center

and outer edges of red, orange and yellow,

stands out against the heated rock surrounding it.

Here the Creator is on display,

wielding his brush on his exquisite palette.

Large herds of bison, once near extinction,
now roam the grasslands in grand numbers,
keeping company with deer, bighorn sheep, wolves,
and the many other forms of wildlife.
The small town of Jackson Hole
gives a peek into the Wild West of bygone days.
This glorious land was once home to Native Americans,
who treasured it as sacred and life-giving.
Their imprint is being carved into the immense
stone statue of Crazy Horse whose face is much larger
than any on Mount Rushmore.
Decades in the formation, it remains a work in progress.
Restoring dignity and honor to a forgotten people
needs to be set in stone for all to see.

Beyond Yellowstone lie the Badlands of South Dakota.
Here large eroded buttes and pinnacles
cover the landscape in shades of gray and sandstone.
It's an eerie sight, stark, yet beautiful.
The solid rock formations are testament
to the resilience of the Sioux,
who once roamed here and paid it homage.
Lost to them, it remains embedded in their heritage.
We celebrated our 50th anniversary in Yellowstone,

my husband and I, arriving just before the perilous pandemic

enveloped our world in its ruthless tentacles,

giving one more reason to count our blessings.

Yellowstone is part of our enduring treasure chest.

PLACE OF RED ROCK

Sedona, Arizona is unique unto itself.

Red sandstone formations glow in brilliant orange and red,

when illuminated by the rising or setting sun.

Red-rock buttes, steep canyon walls and pine forests,

all make their mark here upon the landscape.

One of the most famous sights is the Chapel of the Holy Cross.

Rising 70 feet out of a 1000 foot red-rock cliff,

its most prominent feature is the cross.

Inside is a chapel built some years later

containing a window with benches and pews.

Here one can sit and reflect upon

the magnificent artwork rendered here.

The Creator has painted Sedona in flaming colors,

using his palette to the utmost perfection.

Uptown Sedona is dense with New Age shops,

spas and art galleries along with many fine restaurants.

I spent time hiking along the trails when visiting there,

absorbing the grand scenery and appreciating its

wonder.

Near Sedona lies the epic Grand Canyon,

which I had visited many years earlier.

I still recall looking out over that immense area,

standing in awe of its total grandeur.

Given my fear of heights, I declined riding a mule,

down steep trails to reach the bottom,

which is home to the Hopi Indian reservation.

Sedona is just one of many marvels,

which grace our nation, needing our care and respect.

We are the keepers of these lasting treasures,

And hold the key to their promised future.

EUROPEAN ADVENTURES

I am thankful we traveled abroad when we did,

not waiting until our later years

when getting around would have been difficult.

There is a time and a place for everything,

and we chose the right time.

Our first three-week land tour

gave us a panoramic view of Western Europe.

Traveling by bus through the countryside,

we got a real taste of what each place was like.

Each city we visited is forever painted upon our memories:

Paris, with its unique Haussmann architecture

Rome, with its many ruins dating back to biblical times

Berlin, with its grand opera houses and wonderful bakeries

Venice, with its winding canals and gondola rides

Prague, with its many types of architecture and unique shops

London, with Buckingham Palace, famous Tower and Big Ben

Many other places are stored away as well.

We took cruises aboard large ocean liners,

and a river cruise on a much smaller vessel,

taking us down the Seine in France,

culminating on the beaches of Normandy.

Arriving there on a beautiful sunny day,

it was hard to imagine our troops landing on Omaha Beach,

in wild stormy weather, and although victorious,

suffering countless losses to enemy forces.

We were each given a red rose to place on a grave there.

It puts each Memorial Day more in perspective,

as we honor those who made ultimate sacrifices.

Touring the world makes one truly appreciate God's creation.

He is the true consummate artist,

painting a world to be cared for and treasured by all.

RANDOM THOUGHTS

PERILOUS PANDEMIC

Covid-19 came upon us,

like an inky black river catching us unawares,

morphing into a tsunami of darkness, engulfing our planet,

threatening all we hold dear,

upending lives with overwhelming fear.

Covid-19 came upon us,

and made a mockery of our neglect,

snatching up lives in its spiky molecules,

that we failed to protect.

The tsunami was unrelenting, taking old and young alike:

Doctors and nurses overwhelmed

Patients taking their last breaths alone

Covid-19 came upon us,

and the whole world shuttered,

trying to atone for being blind to its advance,

preferring instead to take a chance,

while the inky black river mocked our fate.

What price ignorance to all that was forewarned?

We tried to make up for being late.

New vaccines promised hope, bringing light into the darkness.

Mankind is forever resilient when facing despair.

Covid-19 came upon us,

catching us in a blind spot with a lesson hard learned,

securing its place in history with its agonizing burn.

RED SKY AT MORNING

September 9th, 2020, was a day to remember.

We woke up to an eerie darkness when it should have been light.

A strange red-orange hue could be seen outside,

glowing in the otherwise darkness.

People were calling it the Apocalypse,

long thought by some to be forthcoming.

It did indeed signal a catastrophic event,

but not the exact end times prophesied by the doomsayers.

For days terrible wildfires had been raging across California,

bought on by drought and lightening strikes.

Thousands of acres and forests were in flames,

destroying homes and claiming lives.

Soot and ash were blotting out the sun,

choking the atmosphere and turning day to night.

Here was climate change painted upon the earth.

Humankind had been the careless artist,

using his palette to create a scene of destruction.

As we gazed in horror upon cities choking on dust,

it still failed to impact upon many the true nature of it all.

We made it through that awful day in September,

knowing all too well that it could be repeated.

Another dry year has been upon us.

The threat of more wildfires is looming.

We can only pray that somehow we will be spared.

Nature is a hard teacher, and we pay for our mistakes,

not being willing to hold ourselves to account,

and make the changes that can determine our future.

Will we truly witness the Apocalypse,

or can we delay its coming for now?

REBUILDING

Our nation's infrastructure needs repair.

It has never been more timely or necessary.

There are numerous potholes on our streets of racial inequality.

There are wide cracks on our highways of immigration reform.

Dangerous bridges loom across areas of gender identity and disability.

Our skies are also not immune, banning travelers

of certain religions, deeming them terrorists.

What will be the cost of our neglect?

Our nation's infrastructure needs repair, and the clock is forever ticking.

Time is quickly running out.

We need the right builders to come together.

So far they remain elusive, hiding in the shadows of disagreement.

Unable to present a united front,

they forever debate, and reach no agreement.

Potholes increase, cracks widen, bridges are

threatened, skies darken.

Our infrastructure may soon be swept away by a great tsunami.

The time is imminent; there is no greater moment.

Our nation's infrastructure cries out for healing.

Where are those in charge with healing?

There is the saying, "Physician heal thyself."

Time has come to heal ourselves, and begin the great task of rebuilding.

Today the sun will rise again on a new morning.

How long will it shine before the clouds roll in?

That's the question our infrastructure demands.

That's the question we need to answer.

COMMUNING WITH THE EARTH

Gardening can be a great way to commune with nature.
I have always enjoyed digging in the ground,
and feeling the soil when planting a garden.
For many years we had a large one
out back along a side fence.
At first there were just some flowers,
including a number of small rose bushes,
which later gave way to a variety of vegetables.
My husband thought it wiser
to plant something we could eat;
thus came tomatoes, peppers, eggplant, zucchini,
garlic, snow peas, onions, Swiss chard, kale,
numerous herbs, and one year even a pumpkin vine.
I'm sure there are others that I have forgotten.

I loved tending the garden, and watching it take shape.
Here, as with the flowers, was painted an array of color.
Nature's palette is always at work,

being the creative artist.

Sometimes there were surprises, the totally unexpected.

A huge zucchini would suddenly appear,

having grown to mammoth size, going unnoticed.

Nature can play some tricks on us.

In later years, we dispensed with the vegetables,

and reverted back to flowers.

Somehow it seemed easier as we aged.

Still there remained the joy of feeling the soil,

communing with it, and appreciating its gift.

Earth is one of our greatest treasures,

meant to be cared for and preserved.

A garden is a good place to start.

SUNSHINE

I have always loved sunshine.

It's a warm furnace on a cold day,

and a sweat-oozing sauna on a hot one,

nature's way of brightening up the world when things seem dark.

When I was young I loved to stretch out beneath its rays,

letting them seep into my skin, and turn it to a golden tan,

never admitting to the danger those rays could bring.

Again youth is immortal; age spots and worse will never occur.

The sun is to be sucked up with abandon.

The future remains at the time obscure.

Time has taught me that too much sunshine may not be a gift.

The earth is heating up under relentless climate change.

Drought prevails over much of our land,

drying, cracking it, turning it to sand.

The world is acquiring an unquenchable thirst,

as the sun bakes it in a forever hotter oven.

Still I love the sunshine that paints the hills in vivid colors,

and creates a rainbow across a stormy sky,

or paints a sunset on a western horizon,

intermingling hues of red and gold.

Beauty and ugliness go hand-in-hand, as do joy and sorrow.

Sunshine brings hope for a new tomorrow,

as long as there is some rain now and then to refresh our world.

Life as we know it requires both, and our need to embrace each one.

I have always loved the sunshine,

but have learned to accept the clouds when they roll in,

being grateful for all that nature brings to its table,

and standing in awe of its incredible bounty, its blessed gifts.

WINDY DAYS

Winds can be fierce along Humboldt County's Lost Coast,

churning up the ocean and sending waves crashing against the rocks.

Water can splash over the jetties,

knocking the careless sightseer out to sea,

never to be seen again.

Winds can indeed be fierce along with mighty storms.

Fishermen brave them, stealing themselves against countless dangers,

with memorial plaques paying tribute to those lost.

The lighthouse at Trinidad, and the huge rock by its harbor,

have seen waves crashing over them,

in a storm from years gone by.

I dislike cold windy days, days that chill me to the bone,

making my eyes water and face go numb.

Warm winds mess up my hair, and are an irritation.

But then again, I recall needing wind to fly a kite,

and watching it soar high into the sky propelled by

wind.

I was a child then, and children are more tolerant,
not concerned with the cold or messy hair.
Wind is a constant presence along the Lost Coast.
Calm mornings morph into unsettled afternoons.
The winds grow stronger with each passing hour.
Trees can fight to hold onto their branches,
which can bend and break in the relentless wind.

In a way I envy those who like windy days,
not minding it blowing through their hair,
or stealing a hat from their head.
What's a little wind after all?
Can it be the Creator's way of blowing off steam,
watching how we humans defy him at every turn?
Windy days can subdue us, and make us mindful
of something greater than ourselves.
Knowing that makes me more respectful of windy days,
but I still don't have to like them.

THOUGHTS ON A RAINY DAY

I have never been a rainy day fan.

Living in California means more sun,

but drought can mean scorching wildfires and loss of life,

so I need to bone up, and welcome the rain.

Nature has a way of playing tricks on us.

Some areas in our world get far too much rain, others not enough.

Dry, cracked deserts are paired with horrific floods.

Both wreck havoc, and cause immense suffering.

Drenching monsoons and terrifying hurricanes,

destroy homes and upend lives.

I well recall the storms in Ohio where I grew up.

In summer there would be steamy humidity drenching one in sweat.

We knew a storm was coming when the sky became coal black.

Suddenly it would become eerily quiet, no bird or animal sounds.

Then would come the wind, followed by sheets of rain,

pelting down sideways, and obscuring all vision.

Maybe hail would fall, hammering against the house,

bouncing off the pavement as it danced to and fro.

Lightening would streak across the sky,

followed by loud cracks of thunder,

causing me to cover my ears, and cower in my room.

Fear of tornadoes was always present,

but I never witnessed one in Ohio.

I had to come to CA for that, and see a small one strike here.

Nature has a way of playing tricks on us.

We never know what we may have to fear.

On a rainy day I can watch the wetness sink into the earth,

and be grateful for nature's welcome drink

of much-needed water for our thirsty land.

Even though I prefer the sun, rain must come when it can,

and I need above all to be its fan!

FEAR OF HEIGHTS

I've had a lifelong fear of heights.
As a child I climbed up to a tree house in a neighbor's yard.
It took courage to make the assent,
but there was no way I was going to descend.
My mother came, and somehow I made it back down.
I no longer recall how, but have a grateful memory.
I marvel at how people can climb to great heights.
Workers walk over rooftops with ease.
They cross over high beams doing construction.
I'm sure I would lose my balance doing such in no time.

I recall an escalator in the metro station in DC.
Coming upon it was like looking into oblivion.
It was the steepest one I had ever seen.
People at the bottom looked like tiny ants scurrying around,
and I stood frozen at the top.
I managed to step on, but then had to sit down for the

duration,

amazed to see others not even holding on, leaning against the side.

For me it was for certain one perilous ride!

Ascending high up in a gondola when in the Grand Tetons,

left me unable to move when it reached the top.

A good Samaritan helped me off,

but just looking down left me weak in the knees.

Other brave souls were climbing up even higher once outside,

and I became dizzy just looking at them.

I do best on terra firma.

I haven't been able to use an escalator for some years now.

I have painted a dark picture of it on my mind's canvas.

I guess most people may have some sort of phobia.

I have learned to cope with mine, doing what my mind will allow.

THE LOVE OF READING

I have always loved to read.
Books paint images on the mind's canvas,
and open windows onto endless landscapes.
My earliest memories are of the "Dick and Jane" readers,
now long abandoned by the public schools.
Being ill as a child meant staying home,
and pouring through two large volumes of fairy tales,
which belonged to my mother.
There I would be transmitted into other worlds,
which often taught valuable lessons.

There was one about the old fisherman,
who caught a large fish that begged him to be set free.
In return the fish would grant a special wish.
Upon his return home to his miserable shack,
the fisherman's wife demanded that he return,
and ask the fish for a nicer place.
So he did, but his wife's demands for even more

resulted in his returning home to "his ditch again."
Ask for too much and wind up with nothing.
How many have fallen into this trap?

I only wish I had saved these books,
but they were lost when I became an adult.
I can recall many favorite characters from books:
Scarlett O'Hara, Huck Finn, Ma and Tom Joad,
to name just a few.
Today there are some books I would no longer read.
Some have been removed from library shelves.
Truly great literature remains to be loved forever.

There is an art to good writing,
to being able to create characters,
that come alive for us and evolve before our eyes.
I have always wanted to write a novel,
but it has remained beyond my reach.
I've had bits and pieces of the puzzle,
but have never been able to lock them all together.
I leave that to others who are such artists,
those who can paint with true colors and ignite the mind
to forever craving even more.

MORE THOUGHTS ABOUT RAIN

We were supposed to get a lot of rain last weekend,
but like many other times recently it didn't arrive.
A little fell overnight and sparsely during the day,
but for the most part it stayed away,
refusing to make its presence known.
We used to get more rain in Humboldt County.
Fog and wet days were much the norm,
and people would head inland to soak up sun.
Too much gray was painted on the weather's canvas.
Lately more yellow sun has replaced gray clouds.
Rain is Nature's way of gifting a thirsty land,
sometimes offering too much, sometimes too little.
Sadly now it is often far too little.

Drought is becoming prevalent in many areas.
Wildfires are a constant threat and source of fear,
Robbing us of all that we hold dear.
Homes and lives have been lost to the specter of climate change.

Humankind has failed to take notice, preferring denial.

We can't admit that we have been the cause,

refusing to take blame.

Old habits die hard, and we fight against changes.

It's easier to look the other way, ignoring the dangers.

Rain is vital to preserving our world and all that is in it.

Even though I have always preferred the sun,

I have to take joy in seeing rain fall and using my umbrella,

knowing that rain is a true gift which seems in short supply,

but nevertheless a treasure upon which we truly rely.

STARGAZING

Before my husband and I were married,

we spent time stargazing in a field near my childhood home.

Lying on the grass, we would look up

at a dark sky filled with stars and constellations,

glittering like jewels on black velvet.

Sometimes we heard cattle mooing in the distance.

Out there we could marvel at the universe,

being far too immense for us to comprehend.

Here the Creator designed one of his greatest mysteries.

Scientists have tried to unlock the answers,

but much remains hidden.

Perhaps that is the way it should be;

not knowing everything makes us human.

Many people are fascinated by outer space,

and the thought of traveling to other planets.

I have no desire to do so; staying on Earth is fine with me.

I admire those who want to land on the Moon or Mars,
daring to travel thousands of miles through space,
maybe never coming home again.
They embrace danger as a means to an end,
seeking answers and finding new realms.
Our hobby of stargazing was short lived.
I barely can name any of the constellations or stars,
gleaming in the night sky, lighting up the darkness.
But I can appreciate all the wonderment painted there,
by a far greater artist than I.

FRIENDSHIPS

Friendships can be one of a person's greatest treasures.

A true friend accepts you for who you are with all your flaws.

Such a friend transcends political and religious differences,

and finds common ground.

A true friend is there for you, always looking out for your back,

refraining from being critical of whatever you may lack.

Fortunate is the one who has many such friends,

but even one or two are a great blessing,

and should be held close to one's heart.

My longest friendship goes back 70 years,

and we have only seen each other once since our early twenties.

But we have remained in touch, sharing about our lives,

while avoiding topics about which we might well differ.

My friends are scattered far and wide,

yet they are the glue that holds my life in stride.

I have them painted as I remember them on my mind's canvas.

We have all changed through the years as we know from looking at pictures from early days.

Ideas may have changed as well,

but true friends rise above that, and hold fast to what is important:

To not stand in judgment

To not give advice when not requested

To be a good listener, and lend support through trials

These are things a true friend does without expecting anything in return.

We meet many people throughout life,

making small talk with them at parties or in other situations.

True friends do not engage in small talk, but get to the root of things.

They dig deep into the soil, find the root, and help bring it to flower.

They apply the fertilizer that is needed to grow a vibrant plant,

praying for one another though the worst of times,

and celebrating with them through the best.

I will always treasure my friendships,

knowing that my life is forever richer because of them.

THE JOY OF GIFTING

Downsizing can be challenging,

especially for the older generation.

Years of collecting furniture, artwork and nick-knacks,

which hold treasured memories painted upon the mind's canvas,

can be difficult to part with,

causing anxiety and even depression.

Upon leaving our home of fifty years,

we confronted the issue of downsizing.

Not wanting to hold an estate or garage sale,

I decided to gift away many things.

There is a joy in gifting, in knowing where your things are.

Paintings now hang in friends' homes.

Rugs lie upon their floors.

Our grandfather clock chimes away in another place.

Furniture, dishes, vases and other items,

also found new homes with our many friends.

It was my way of thanking them,

letting them know that they were valued.
I still have more than enough remaining
to remind me of a lifetime of blessings.
Gifting can bring a sense of peace,
and a chance to paint a new picture.
Moving forward cannot happen until letting go.
That can happen through the joy of gifting.

STUFF OF DREAMS

Why do we dream?

I have read there are many reasons why we enter the world of dreams which can paint a picture that may or may not mirror reality.

Some dreams are pleasant, and we are sorry to wake up,

wishing we could venture on, keeping them on our mind's canvas.

Others may evoke terror, causing us to awaken in a sweat.

In rare cases one may sleepwalk, opening doors,

with no recollection on the morning after.

Some dreams can be universal:

Running in slow motion

Trying to find a classroom

Realizing that one has never attended a required course

Attempting to solve a problem

The sensation of falling

Do dreams mirror reality?

Many people think they do.

What may be happening during our waking hours,

may well take place in dreams.

That's when the final painting in both realms can be completed.

The colors of reality can be augmented in our dreams.

Lately I've questioned whether what I thought was a dream

was actually a true event.

Was I really in these locations, or did I simply dream about them?

The mind can play tricks on us, coloring things one way,

and then adding a different shade to alter the picture.

My dreams have become less vivid as I age.

Most times I know I have had a dream, but upon waking,

the canvas is wiped clean, and no colors remain.

Still there are those rare times when the dream painting

retains its vivid hues, and I know that dreaming has not been lost.

Dreaming is one of life's mysteries which may always remain hidden,

despite our desire to know everything in this world.

And the question remains, should we?

INTERNET CONNECTIONS

It was once known as the Information Super Highway.
Like a massive infrastructure it completely changed our lives.
Nothing would ever be the same.
Computers came to rule our world, shrinking it in size,
as our world became connected,
every nation intertwined.
Gone were the old typewriters with no spell check.
Gone were the libraries with their card catalogues,
now replaced by Google Search.

Anything can be found online.
Amazon has lived up to its name.
Many stores have vanished like straws in the wind.
Our world is a more dangerous place.
Very little of our lives remain sacred.
Identity theft is rampant; scams abound.
Cyberbullying torments young people,
sometimes with disastrous results.

We have become a "watch your back" society.

Technology has come to rule our lives

like a great spider catching us in its web.

We can admire the web's beauty and intricate design,

until its sticky threads engulf us and our sensibilities ebb.

Would we turn back the clock to a former time?

Would we give up all we have gained along this Super Highway?

Youth would definitely say no, along with many far older.

We want to stay connected even if the price is high.

Like all things in life, there is little turning back.

Our internet will keep changing, forever becoming more complex.

We humans can't stand still, such is our nature.

Life is all too short which is its amazing trait.

Such is Mankind, to ever advance is his fate.

REUNIONS REVISITED

I was not that popular in high school.
I never dated, and never went to my senior prom.
I got my recognition from being an honor student
And playing the violin.
I spent my time studying instead to going to parties.
I grew up quickly, attaining my adult height
of five feet eight inches by the time I was twelve.
Until the ninth grade I always was in the back row
for the yearly school picture.

Growing up I was far more reserved than now.
I was the only child of older parents.
My mother had a full-term still birth at age 38,
a boy my parents named Thomas Robert.
I can only imagine the grief they felt,
and what courage it took to have another child.
I always found it easier to talk to adults,
feeling that my peers were immature.

That all changed after my marriage.
I started feeling comfortable in my skin,
and with my place in life.
Meeting other couples, sharing common experiences,
made me more confident to be with people.
As time passed, I became quite the opposite
of what I was growing up.
Instead of trying to look older, I aimed to look younger.

When I tell people what I was like in my younger years,
most find it hard to believe.
I love meeting new people in unfamiliar surroundings.
I don't wait for people to come up to me first,
and enjoy being the one to initiate a conversation.
Those early years have taught me a lesson,
that we can change and be far better off for it.

Attending my 25th and 40th high school reunions
changed my perspective on my classmates.
Many came up to me, and I could see how they were not the same.
Some who had been very popular back then
were friendly and seemed genuinely interested
in what I had done over the years.

Instead of feeling rejected, I felt accepted.

Reunions for me were a good thing.

My early life pictures were rather drab ones, lacking color.

The ones that followed were far more vibrant.

MY FIFTH APPENDAGE

I have played violin for almost as long as I can remember.

Along with my arms and legs it is like a fifth appendage.

Through the years we have had a Jekyll and Hyde relationship,

with my loving to play in groups but disliking to practice.

Unfortunately playing the violin requires practice,

many hours of it if one is to play well.

My teacher was of the old school, and music was her life.

So I took two lessons a week in the summer,

and was supposed to practice at least two hours a day.

I was lucky to practice one.

How I dreaded the long drawn out recitals,

waiting my turn to play my memorized piece,

hands clammy, body trembling, terrified of going on stage.

Recitals were held in an art gallery with my father as

my accompanist.

He could understand my stage fright as he suffered from the same.

Knees shaking caused the bow to tremble across the strings,

sending me into a veritable panic, terrified that I would forget the notes.

I've never since cared to solo, preferring the safety of groups.

The violin is a challenging instrument, and not for the faint of heart.

Pitch depends on the ear of the player, and the tone deaf need not apply.

My fifth appendage has suffered over the years.

Rotator cuff tears and tendon ruptures from other exercise,

have taken an unfortunate toll.

After more than sixty years I now struggle to play,

but the will is still there as I confront the unrelenting Mr. Hyde.

Eventually he will get the best of me,

but for right now I'm keeping him at bay.

MISSED MY CALLING?

For many decades swimming was my passion.

So much so that at times I thought I might have missed my calling,

and should have been born a fish!

I really can't remember when I didn't swim.

Gliding through the water weightless,

able to turn backward flips, stand on my hands,

all the things I could never do on land.

There I was awkward, clumsy,

at the mercy of my stiff joints,

never limber like I was in the water.

For years I swam at least two miles a day and often more,

rarely missing a day even in bad weather.

Rain, cold, even hail didn't stop me from owning the water.

Feeling a mass of goose bumps attack my skin

as I hurried to dive into the pool to escape the wind,

churning out endless laps, sometimes wearing fins,

yes, I should have been born a fish!

Swimmers tend to be territorial, seeking out a particular lane line and claiming it theirs.

I had my favorite, but it was not set in stone.

Sometimes giving way a bit can be the better choice.

Pools seemed safer than open water,

where frigid temperature and dangerous currents could be an undoing.

Plus I always liked to know what was on the bottom.

Then in later years I had the first of many rotator cuff tears.

Swimming became more difficult,

until I was reduced to just treading water.

Life teaches us many lessons.

One can always overdo a good thing and pay the price.

I no longer think I missed my calling.

I wasn't meant to be a fish in the grand scheme of things,

but it was wonderful while it lasted.

PEDDLING AWAY

I fondly remember my biking days,

peddling away through neighborhood streets or down trails.

Biking was yet another way of combating anxiety,

meditating or communing with nature.

How vivid the colors were painted on my mind's canvas,

before they turned a darker hue as age and fear set in.

Once again youth has no sense of danger

of falling off or being hit by a car.

For years I biked long distances, aware of traffic, but not ruled by it.

Slowly small increments of gray fear replaced courage.

Traffic suddenly seemed closer, more threatening.

Even mundane bike trails became a challenge.

No matter where I was I could always fall off,

and life might never be the same.

I knew of people, hardcore cyclists, who suffered injury,

and marveled that some could still mount a bike.

Such could not be the case with me.

After many glorious years, my bike sat parked in the garage,

tires going flat, and frame gathering dust.

Then came the day when it was gone forever,

and my days of peddling away were just a memory,

of the days when biking, and all its joy were a must.

ON TURNING 75

Father Time came knocking at my door.

I don't recall inviting him to visit,

but there he was on my doorstep demanding to come in.

Like a generous guest he came bearing gifts:

White hair

 Stooped shoulders

 Sagging skin,

 Age spots

All the signs of growing older

He was in no hurry to depart,

continuing to reside and leave his mark.

Like a down and out friend, he prepared to stay indefinitely,

working his way as he pleased.

No boundaries could be set.

No way for him to have regret.

He has found his place with me.

Little did I know when I was young
that he would trap me in his net.
Age creeps up like a silent thief,
and things are stolen one-by one,
before we realize what's been done.
Getting older is part of life,
and no one escapes its forward march.
Acceptance comes with moving ahead,
not looking back, but forging on.
Father Time is not a welcome guest,
but we can live with him nevertheless.
No matter how weak the body may become,
the soul can remain forever strong.
Father Time came knocking at my door,
and will always stay with me.
Accepting that is the key.

REFLECTIONS ON A MARRIAGE

We met on a blind date in 1967.
Tony's college roommate at Ohio State,
and my sorority sister who would be his future wife
brought us together to go on a hay ride.
I still recall how Tony stood at the bottom of the stairs
at my sorority house looking up at me,
smiling as I descended the steps.

It was the beginning of a two-year courtship
during which we discovered our love of music.
Tony had a large record collection,
including almost everything Beethoven had ever written.
Our love of music, Italian food and biking
were just some of the many things we shared.

Our courtship was not all smooth sailing.

I had my fears about marriage, and what it would mean.

Dark colors appeared on my mind's canvas.

Marriage is a life changing event.

Was I ready to make this giant leap into the unknown?

At one point I called the wedding off and gave back the ring.

Fortunately I changed my mind, and we got back on track.

Our wedding was simple by many of today's standards.

We were married on a hot, steamy Ohio afternoon

in my parents' long time church with no air-conditioning.

There was cake and punch after the ceremony,

followed by a picnic-style buffet at my parents' home

attended by the wedding party and relatives.

Tony and I left early for our honeymoon,

spending our first night in Zanesville, Ohio,

before traveling to Williamsburg, Virginia.

After visiting other historic sites, including Washington DC,

we returned to Tony's home in Lebanon, PA

for a gathering there of friends and relatives

who could not attend the wedding.

Once we said our vows and walked back down the isle,

a peace came over me, and I knew that I had done the right thing.

The dark colors of earlier changed to bright ones.

Ours is a testament to the love we have for one another.

Tony is my soulmate and my best friend.

He was there for me during my parents' final years,

lending support to my mother once Dad was gone.

He was right by my side during two surgeries,

always ready to lend a hand,

and likewise was the same after our daughter's birth.

Our marriage is a treasure that is all too fleeting now days.

At a time when so many marriages fail almost from the start,

ours has endured the test for time, and grown ever stronger.

I don't recall much about that hayride,

but it led to something wonderful.

Together we have painted lasting memories.

MUFFIN

She showed up by surprise on our doorstep

many years ago when our daughter was just eleven,

tiny dark gray ball of fur with traces of black and orange.

She followed our daughter to school and back that day,

obviously determined to become part of our family.

She would live with us for the next 21 years,

becoming close buddies with our other cat Taffy.

Days would find them curled up together on the ironing board,

or outside on the back patio.

Muffin loved to keep our daughter company,

lying next to her on the bed and giving her a paw massage.

She grew substantial in her middle years,

as she never turned down a meal or treat.

Her bosom companion Taffy had a sudden seizure,

right before Thanksgiving and crossed the Rainbow Bridge,

where all loyal pets go when the time comes.

She was 15, just a few months older than Muffin.

Muffin was nowhere ready to give up any of her nine lives.

At 16 we feared we might lose her to kidney disease,

but she had other ideas, and proved us wrong.

I always said when she stopped eating that was a sign,

and finally the day came when that happened.

By then she had shrunk to a shadow of her former self.

I found her lying between the washer and water heater,

resting peacefully and preparing to leave her home of 21 years.

Always one to sound off with loud meows when heading to the vet,

this time she made no sound; there was absolute silence.

She was almost gone when she got the injection,

lying on a pretty little cloth with our tears to keep her company.

We had her cremated, and kept her ashes in a little cedar box,

until the day came to bury them.

Our daughter had long since moved away,

but was home for a visit, and the time seemed appropriate.

For years after, we had a statue placed there in remembrance.

I kept the small piece of her fur that we got from the vet

safely stored with the family bible,

until I framed it, and gave it to our daughter as a gift.

Muffin endeared herself to us from the moment she arrived

until she took her last breath.

She was special indeed, and we were fortunate to have had her.

We like to think of her as scampering free,

just beyond the Rainbow Bridge, and never turning down any treats,

KEEPING THE FAITH

KEEPING THE FAITH

Years ago I never thought much about mortality.
Heaven forbid I would look at the obituaries.
Time moved more slowly when I was young,
and fifty years seemed like an eternity, let alone seventy-five.
Even seeing my grandfather in his coffin when I was eleven,
did not have the finality of seeing my parents in theirs.
Lately I have been thinking more about the hereafter.
It's a matter of becoming better in touch with my faith,
and in better communication with God.

In some ways this has been easier during the pandemic,
which started turning our lives upside down in 2020.
I could no longer attend church in person,
and didn't find virtual services that effective.
Prayer has been more prominent now than in the past,
having grown on me more with the passing years.
I truly believe that my prayers are answered,
even though this might not happen exactly when or

how.

Things have a way of working together for good.

I've never been a good student of the Bible.

I find much of it difficult to read.

The Old Testament deals with an angry and vengeful God,

which I find hard to reconcile with a loving one.

The full impact of God's sacrifice in the New Testament,

still remains a mystery which I have yet to explore.

I focus on the salvation message which is simple, yet complex.

Maybe I don't need to understand it all, just take it and be grateful.

How old is our universe?

Scientists say billions of years, not a mere six thousand.

Much life seemed to come well before Adam and Eve.

No mention is made of the dinosaurs or other ancient life forms.

Can evolution be part of God's plan?

Given the wonder of the universe I see no reason why not.

Adam and Eve could be His final perfection of mankind.

I see no reason why they cannot be set apart with no

missing link,

total separation here from anything which came before.

Even though parts of the Bible may seem unbelievable,

the Bible to me is an intrical part of Christianity.

The two cannot be separated even though we have a right to question.

The more I study it, the more I may come to understand.

What's most important is knowing that God is there for me,

and just as He answers prayers,

He may well teach me more important lessons,

further opening my eyes, and helping me to see.

He is the ultimate artist, painting his wondrous design on my mind's canvas.

The colors are radiant and glowing as I further grow and come to believe.

ONE CHILD

Eyes not seeing, ears not hearing, lying sideways upon your mat,

what do you see, what do you hear?

Do you have some internal light, some internal sound?

Lying sideways upon your mat

Living, breathing, forever seizing

Waiting for calm between the storms

Other lives are put on hold.

Dreams shattered and all that mattered

Consumed by guilt, consumed by sorrow

And all hope for tomorrow

Your life remains a mystery.

No questions answered; no solutions found.

Eyes not seeing, ears not hearing, what is your purpose?

There is a season.

There is a purpose to all things under heaven.

What is your purpose?

If God doesn't make mistakes, why you?

Answers require ascending high mountains.

There are many hazards along the way, many needs for respite.

Answers only come in a final peace of acceptance.

Eyes not seeing, ears not hearing, lying sideways upon your mat,

are you still there, or are you in a new realm forever free?

A DARK PLACE

I am eleven when I see the picture:
two small girls, one grotesquely swollen, the other normal.
"Identical twins until nephrosis struck,"
reads the caption on the flier about kidney disease.
I am eleven, and I am entering a dark place.

Suddenly I'm consumed by fear.
Is this to be my fate?
Images on UNICEF films in Sunday school:
Kwashiokor, elephantiasis, yaws, leprosy
Pouring over library books, horrified by pictures
I am eleven, and I am in a dark place.

My grandfather is dying.
I see him lying in his bedroom, mouth open, eyes unseeing.
I see him at the funeral parlor surrounded by flowers.
I will never forget the smell of funeral flowers.
I am eleven, and I am in a dark place.

How can I live to be fifty?

Fifty to me was old.
Thoughts of escape enter my mind.
I am at the swimming pool.
Should I hold my head under water?
What other realm would await me?
Would I find peace or even more fear?

I am eleven, and at a church.
Mother and I are there for a rummage sale.
I see a chapel, and decide to enter.
I am on my knees saying my childlike prayer.
I suddenly feel a presence, but no one is there.
Gradually I feel the dark place turn to light,
and I feel a peace.
Something has touched me:
The Holy Spirit, and I am forever changed.

POETIC MEMOIR

Why do people write a memoir?
It seems to be a rite of passage as one ages,
trying to leave a legacy for future generations.
We don't want to be forgotten by those we've left behind.
Great composers live on through their music,
artists through their art, authors through their writings.
Most lives are more mundane,
far less notable, but still valued.
They also need to be remembered,
and so the need for a memoir.

I never thought much about doing a memoir,
but then realized that my poetry could be one.
Through my poems I have recalled places,
events and thoughts about things,
trying to paint a picture through poems on my life's canvas.
Even though few people may read them,
they are there nevertheless, a brief chronicle of my earthly existence.

I have had many blessings over the years,

along with some regrets which can't be erased.

Life is a series of hills and valleys with plateaus in between.

We take the good along with the bad,

and try to find serenity in what cannot be changed.

All smooth sailing might not be that interesting.

Adversity can make us grow stronger if we meet it head-on.

No human being is perfect; we all fall short.

I long ago embraced prayer as my true support.

Nothing else can take its place,

But holding onto faith at times can be a challenge,

and I always have to work at that.

So herein, I leave my memoir,

a little piece of me for all who desire to can see.

ONE FINAL THOUGHT

Many people think we are now in the end times.
Global warming, endless wars and conflict,
worldwide pandemics and terrible suffering,
all seem to paint a dark and foreboding picture.
Sometimes I think I am glad to be as old as I am,
but my fear lies with future generations
who will reap what the past ones have created.

I still like to believe there is hope,
that a brighter picture can be painted
on my mind's canvas, a more colorful one.
I am a firm believer in prayer,
being more so as the years advance.
My prayers are not always answered
in the exact time and way I want them to be,
but in the end they always work together for good.

Even though the Earth has billions of people,
I still believe there is a power great enough
to be there for me.
How else can one explain this wondrous creation,

this vast universe stretching beyond comprehension?
Lately I've been spending more time
thinking about what lies ahead, here and beyond.

I hope I will be making my last move
to a new and far better place.
However I've never liked moving,
and leaving here will be the furthest move of all.
Despite all its troubles, Earth is still a wondrous place.
I have seen a lot of it, but wish I could see more.

I would never want to remain here forever,
but wish I could choose the time to leave.
These poems are my legacy, my memoir.
I like to think that in the end
I will have run a good race, stayed the course,
and kept the faith.

ACKNOWLEDGMENTS

I am deeply indebted to the following people who were instrumental in my writing this book:

Tony Jennetti for his invaluable assistance in helping with publishing

Theresa Jennetti for her assistance in editing

Karl Kadie, Carol Korzow and Katharine Wilson for critiquing my poems and offering helpful suggestions, and to both Karl and Carol for guiding me through the publishing process

My longtime friend and former neighbor, Jeanette Lavoie, author of *The Bread Lady's Quest*, who encouraged me in my writing and put me in contact with the artist Gigi Whitt

My very talented artist, Gigi Whitt, who designed the cover for my book

ABOUT THE ARTIST

Gigi Whitt who designed both the front and back cover of this book in addition, was born in the Philippine Islands. She is a graduate of the Philippine Women's University where she majored in Fine Art's-Advertising. To quote her, she says, "Through acrylics, dyes and watercolors, I depict the most colorful spring of life. I am always searching for a way to transpose my thoughts and feelings to the canvas, to share to others a sense of wholeness and harmony, especially the harmony of color. I look to my personal experiences, travel, reading and nature for inspiration, then portray numerous layers of emotions with each brushstroke, resulting in grand floral escapes and landscapes on my canvas."

Gigi currently lives in Southern California and spends most of her time with family, friends, and creating artwork. She also enjoys teaching young children art and baking. She can be contacted at artinspirations93@gmail.com.

ABOUT THE AUTHOR

MJ Jennetti was born in Michigan, and grew up in Ohio. She graduated from Ohio State University where she majored in English. After teaching briefly at the secondary level, she spent most of her career working in special education. In addition to writing poetry, her interests include playing the violin, reading, hiking and working out at her gym. She and her husband have lived in California for over fifty years, and currently reside in Eureka near their daughter. *Painting With Poetry* is her first book.

www.ingramcontent.com/pod-product-compliance
Lightning Source LLC
Chambersburg PA
CBHW022018290426
44109CB00015B/1223